MORE FROM A BOOK APART

Color Accessibility Workflows
Geri Coady

Making Sense of Color Management
Craig Hockenberry

Working the Command Line
Remy Sharp

Pricing Design
Dan Mall

Get Ready for CSS Grid Layout
Rachel Andrew

Visit abookapart.com for our full list of titles.

Publisher: Jeffrey Zeldman
Designer: Jason Santa Maria
Executive Director: Katel LeDû
Editor: Lisa Maria Martin
Technical Editor: Kirupa Chinnathambi
Copyeditor: Kate Towsey
Proofreader: Katel LeDû
Book Producer: Ron Bilodeau

ISBN: 978-1-937557-59-1

A Book Apart
New York, New York
http://abookapart.com

TABLE OF CONTENTS

FOREWORD

WHEN I FIRST SAW *Toy Story* in 1995, I immediately knew I wanted to be an animator. Years later, I went to college for it, where I learned a lot—including the fact that, although I liked animation, it didn't like me back. I took, and enjoyed, classes that talked to me about squash and stretch, anticipation, secondary actions, and all the principles that drew me to cartoons and movies in the first place. But I just didn't like *being* an animator.

Luckily, I stumbled into a blossoming field then called "interactive design." I finished school with knowledge of typography and HTML and Flash and white space, and spent the next decade designing websites instead of animations. During that same time, Flash animation was gratuitously used and abused, often getting in the way of what people actually wanted to do on the web—and giving digital animation as a whole a bad name.

Then the iPhone came out.

Suddenly, we realized that animation isn't just a nice-to-have; it can actually help us. It can show us where things come from and where things go. It can calm us down and excite us. We've now seen the value of animation in interface design, and we're primed to integrate it into our own work.

If words and phrases like "animatics" or "frame rates" aren't familiar to you, have no fear: this book will get you up to speed in no time. Rachel's thorough approach doesn't just tell you what animation is but, more importantly, why it works. She'll show you how brains and eyes work, the historical context of web animation, tips for collaborating with colleagues to get the work done, and much more.

Without further ado, welcome to animation at work.

—Dan Mall

To Joe, the best cheerleader and support crew I could ask for.

INTRODUCTION

BEFORE I WORKED IN WEB DEVELOPMENT, I was an award-winning cartoonist. I always wanted to see my comics moving on a screen—but I ended up moving interfaces on a screen instead!

It was a long journey to get from telling stories with words and pictures to sharing other people's stories with code and pixels. And, at first, I struggled to explain the importance of purposeful animation, to justify expending effort on it to stakeholders burned by Flash. This is the book I wish I'd had when I started.

This is not a book about what JavaScript library to use, how to write CSS transitions, or how to create performant animations with browser developer tools. There are a great many wonderful books about those topics already.

What this book *does* contain is distilled, timeless advice on why animation matters and when to put it to use on the web: where to incorporate it into designs, how to communicate it across teams with different skillsets, and how to implement it responsibly. My intention is for this book to empower you and your teammates to make informed, long-term decisions about what to animate—or not animate.

It answers all the questions bosses, clients, and workshop attendees have asked me about UI animation over the years. It shines a light on the things we do know, and—perhaps most crucially—it points out what we don't know. (And there's a *lot* we don't know.)

Before we go too far, let me clear up some terminology. We are bandying about the terms "motion design" and "UI animation" and "web animation" a lot these days. Sometimes we even use them synonymously! But there are some big differences worth clarifying.

- *Animation* is the act of changing something—animating it. Animation is not limited to motion: you can change something's color or opacity or even morph it into a new shape without moving it.
- *Motion design* is a branch of animation and/or graphic design, depending on your perspective. You could say that motion

design is to animation what graphic design is to illustration: the latter serves as a form of expression and communication, storytelling, and art, whereas the former exists to convey and serve the information it's delivering to its audience. Motion designers create a wide range of animations, from movie credit sequences to interstitials for television news to explainer videos.

- *UI animation* refers to animating user interfaces on any device, from DVD menus to iPhone apps to dropdown menus on the web. Even a light swirling on your smartwatch or a screen wipe on your eInk reader is a kind of UI animation.
- *Web animation* encompasses animation, motion design, and UI animation used on the web. Web animations are implemented with technologies like CSS, HTML, WebGL, SVG, and JavaScript.

To fully understand animation and its implications for the future of web design, we must first examine the roots of animation itself.

The illusion of life

When most folks think of "animation," the first thing to spring to mind is often a cartoon character like Mickey Mouse or Sailor Moon. But those are just examples of animation applied to illustration. Animation itself is a visual representation of change over time. And it has some powerful applications. Applied with precision, it can enrich digital environments and help users make smarter, faster decisions. But, like so many of humankind's greatest tools, before we put animation to work, we used it for entertainment.

In the early 1920s, the popularity of theatres propelled booms in both movie-making and animation. New York advertising firms scrambled to create entertaining ads and bumpers for cinemas around the country, causing animation studios to sprout like weeds. One young man chose to head west and start his own animation studio closer to Hollywood, where housing and labor were cheaper. His name was Walt Disney.

Disney did have rivals and equals—animation giants in their own right, like Chuck Jones of Warner Bros. fame. But Disney outpaced them all. He was a shrewd businessman who fiercely guarded his studio's intellectual property and invested heavily in technology like Technicolor and the multiplane camera that allowed for shooting parallax effects. He made deals to secure international distribution, thus reaching animators and artists across the globe like Osamu Tezuka, who would become the father of Japanese animation.

Some of Disney's "Nine Old Men"—Disney's core animators turned directors—wrote a book about the techniques used under their watch. *The Illusion of Life* contained the "Twelve Principles of Animation" espoused by these animators to help breathe vitality into their illustrations. In the early 1990s, computer scientists began applying these principles to interface design (PDF).

Animation at work

Windows and Macintosh operating systems had been jostling for pole position for years when researchers began studying how animation impacts human computer interaction. Soon, subtle motion design started showing up in both systems, from the "genie effect" in Macs to the "minimize window" animation on Windows machines. Quietly, without fanfare, animation became a core offering for both platforms.

Meanwhile, animation on the web was overt, in your face, experiential, entertaining. Flash plugins enabled games, cartoons, even overblown "flashy intros" users had to sit through before they could access the content. While it did become common courtesy for such sites to provide a "skip intro" button—and many people, myself included, enjoyed the entertainment Flash provided—animation on the web got a reputation for style over substance.

It has been said *so* many times before that I'm loath to say it again, but the iPhone changed everything. Earlier touchscreen interfaces had been attempted, but none had coupled the input of a user's fingertips with immediate, visual feedback—animation. The iPhone's expert use of animation created natural-feeling app interfaces that maximized use of space and responded to users' gestures.

Since then, apps have been influencing many web design trends, down to hamburger menus and horizontal scrolling on websites. And with touchscreens replacing point-and-click interfaces on many devices, users expect the web to look and feel more like apps. The line between "the web" and "app" has blurred so much that we use "web app" to refer to sites that are more than just HTML documents.

For anyone building sites that look, feel, perform, and serve as well as an app, animation is an essential tool. Operating systems, apps, and video games have shown us that animation cannot just differentiate products but must also serve our users. Animation provides critical context and guidance for users flooded with information. It can mask slow performance and even be used to increase perceived performance. Good motion design provides a sheen of polish and branding that can engender users' trust with as much strength as a professional logo. And smart companies are paying attention.

The following chapters are the culmination of my experiences: from consulting with Silicon Valley tech companies to giving workshops around the world to studying studio animation, motion design, and UI animation. I've reached out to animation evangelists, front-end developers, product designers, and UX researchers at companies like Intuit and Etsy to provide that in-house perspective so often missing from books written by consultants.

For some folks, animation is still a dirty word—something decorative to be slapped on at the end of the project if there's enough budget left over, or avoided altogether. But there is power in animation. The power to create experiences that go beyond mere linked documents. The power to immerse users in an illusion of life. And that power is about to be yours.

HUMAN PERCEPTION
AND ANIMATION

WE HAVE A TENDENCY in the web industry to relegate animation to the very last moment in a project's production, tacking it on at the end as a nice-to-have. But animation is so much more than window dressing! UI animation can reduce cognitive load and increase perceived speed for users, giving our projects that competitive edge.

In order to make powerful animations that help users, first we have to learn a little more about the human visual system. Buckle up, because we're about to get science-y!

THE HUMAN VISUAL SYSTEM

We humans have a very special visual processing system. Whereas most mammals' vision is largely motion-based, primates have an additional color component to their vision. This extra component of vision changed our brains as we evolved.

Now consider that we can animate three things:

- **Position or location:** We can move an element in relationship to its surroundings (like sending it across a page); or we can move it in relationship to itself (like making it spin in a circle).
- **Form or shape:** We can change an element's form by scaling its size up or down; or we can fundamentally change its shape into something new, from a triangle to a square.
- **Color:** At its simplest, we can animate an element's transition from one color to the next. We can also change the opacity of a color, which the human eye perceives as a change in density or material.

Conveniently, these three properties translate into two visual processes in our brains (FIG 1.1):

- An older system present even in our most ancient ancestors for tracking location, motion, and physical relationships.
- A newer process for distinguishing things by their properties—like color and shape—that evolved when our primate ancestors acquired color vision.

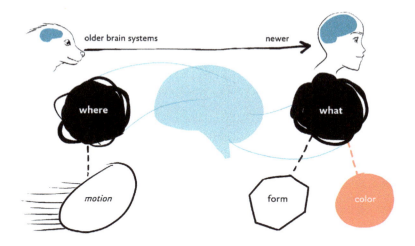

FIG 1.1: The human visual system differs from that of most other mammals: color vision means we're not completely bound to motion like our primitive ancestors, but motion remains a strong and ancient component of how our brains construct our perception of reality.

Margaret Livingstone called these the "Where System" and the "What System" in her book *Vision and Art: The Biology of Seeing,* which I highly recommend to anyone nerdy enough to be reading *this* book.

Interfaces and designs tickle the more recently evolved What System, helping users identify elements on a screen by their shape and color. But when we design with motion, too, we tap into the older Where System. We can use motion to orient users in an information space and shore up spatial hierarchy.

Designing with motion can be very powerful for guiding users. For instance, when a user is navigating through a site, using a sliding motion between pages can help them keep track of where they are in a linear list of items. Motion jacks directly into the Where System, which interfaces with all kinds of orienting mechanisms. Meanwhile, having a list item change colors to indicate its availability will tap into the What System, helping users recognize that an overall state of being has changed.

CUTS AND CONTEXT SWITCHING

Animation can add critical context to seemingly disconnected elements and events. Offloading this context to the visual cortex reduces cognitive load and increases perceived speed. But most websites are built around instantaneous transitions with little to no context.

Consider the simple act of navigating a website: after a user clicks a link, information is painted onto the screen as quickly as possible. If the render time is particularly slow, users might see a flash of white between clicks.

Each time the new page is rendered, users must re-evaluate where they are and their context. Each time, their brains must determine, "Does this page look like the last page I looked at? Yes? Okay, now where is the part that changed..."

A "cut" is a term from cinematography that dates back to when directors would literally cut and splice pieces of film together to connect shots from different angles and shoots to create a narrative. This works well on screen because audiences instinctively watch actors' hands and gaze, which directors can use to connect two disparate shots (**FIG 1.2**). And audiences are trained! It works like a charm.

The web remains largely cut-driven, much to our users' detriment. User interfaces lack faces, hands, and other cues. Sweeping screen changes can be disorienting, while smaller changes might go unnoticed entirely. During testing, we might hear a user sheepishly ask, "What just happened?"

Establishing shot of a man and woman talking.

Cut to the man looking up at the woman.

Cut to what the man sees: the woman looking back.

FIG 1.2: Cuts in film allow the camera to quickly ping-pong between faces in a conversation without motion.

FIG 1.3: This dropdown goes from one state to the other, no animations—just a cut from one to the other.

Early operating systems were entirely cut-based. This was partly because early processors couldn't handle animation, and partly because software was often designed with a "read the manual" mentality. Since then, users have learned to adapt: after clicking on a long box, the box that appears underneath must be a dropdown (**FIG 1.3**). But it still takes quite a bit of mental work and training to get there.

But there are some interactions, whether new to us or ambiguous, that no amount of training or previous experience can prepare us for and no amount of inference can reveal. In these instances, animation adds context that still images and cuts can't give us.

Imagine an image of three spheres in a row—the "before" state—and a second image in which one of the spheres has moved—the "after" state. The after state can be achieved through multiple relationships between the spheres, and each possible relationship changes the meaning of that state (**FIG 1.4**).

Which ball is on the upper right? This important relationship cannot be inferred without animation (or judicious amounts of color coding, labeling, and explanatory text—which generally makes for a cumbersome design!). Even if we did use a diagram or a second color to clarify, our users would still waste time having to decode the information on the screen.

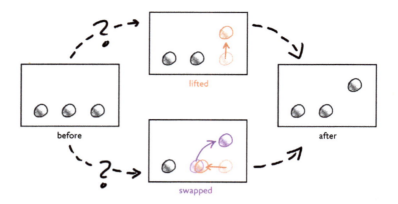

FIG 1.4: There are many ways to achieve the same after state, but only by animating the process will the true nature of the spheres' relationship become crystal clear.

Alternatively, if we make the relationship explicit through animation, that's time users can spend thinking about what to do next, not *What just happened?* And it's all thanks to the magic of the brain's visual cortex.

THE HIGH ROAD THROUGH THE BRAIN'S GPU

A cut-based interaction forces the user's brain to imagine all the in-between states that could have been. "In-betweening" comes from animation: it's when an animator takes two key poses (or frames) and draws all the states in between them (**FIG 1.5**).

In-betweening is very time consuming and not very glamorous, so it's often dumped on interns or sent overseas. No one wants to grow up to be an in-betweener: it's a dead-end job. And the human brain doesn't do so great at in-betweening either (**FIG 1.6**). It takes a lot of bandwidth for the brain to connect the dots between cuts. People like you and I—who work on computers day in and day out—have adapted, but new users, casual users,

FIG 1.5: In this sequence of drawings, the extreme left and right cats (in blue) are in "key poses." The grey cats in transitional states between them are "in-between" frames. You may have heard Flash developers refer to these intermediate states as "tweens."

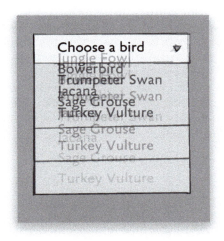

FIG 1.6: When we see a cut in our UI, our brains do the in-betweening for us.

incapacitated users, and folks just not in the mental prime of their life can get snagged on these cognitive bottlenecks.

Fortunately, animation can help. Researchers Scott E. Hudson and John T. Stasko found in the early '90s that sudden changes could distract users (PDF) from what they were doing, and that animation "allows the user to continue thinking about the task domain, with no need to shift contexts to the interface domain. By eliminating sudden visual changes, animation lessens the chance that the user is surprised."

There is research in film narrative that seems to support this as well, indicating that cuts between actions cause a sort of internal reset for the viewer's mental model of what is going on. This aligns with observational evidence that cuts between human interaction and computer reactions are especially disorienting, and helps explain why animation was so crucial to touch interface development.

Let me elaborate. Computers have two processors: one for complex system tasks, the Central Processing Unit (CPU), and the other for tackling the major number-crunching involved in processing and displaying graphics, the Graphics Processing Unit (GPU). In this analogy, because cuts require in-betweening, they get processed on the main thread—what we might call our brain's CPU—where *everything* is processed: from what you are currently doing to what you need to do next to what things you need to pick up at the grocery store tonight. This bogs your cognitive system down and slows reaction times.

Using animation to explicitly show users the in-betweening keeps those processes on the brain's visual cortex instead (**FIG 1.7**). This lets users stay focused and on task. In this way, you can think of animation as a shortcut through the brain's GPU, so to speak.

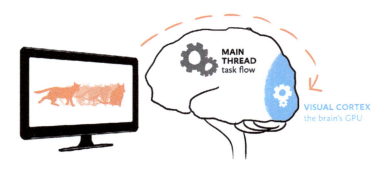

FIG 1.7: Animation lets the visual cortex handle spatial association and content change, freeing up the rest of the brain to stay on task.

THE CONE OF VISION

The human eye is most sensitive to color and details in a very small spot called the foveal region. Meanwhile, our peripheral vision, while blurry and lacking color, is highly sensitive to movement. In fact, on the very outer edges of our retina, it doesn't even transmit visual information to the brain. It only detects movement and sends a signal to jerk our eyes in that direction.

So how are we not living in a blurry monotone world? What we perceive as vision is not actually a one-to-one representation of what we perceive with our eyes. It's more like a simulated picture based on patches of information. You're not aware of it, but your eye moves constantly in *saccades*—tiny, jerky movements that send snapshots of information from different areas back to the brain, letting it repaint and update our picture of the world around us.

These physical realities have real-world ramifications for motion design and animation in web and interface design. For instance, a person cannot focus on two independently moving objects on opposite sides of a screen at the same time. They're also less likely to notice color changes happening in their peripheral vision.

I like to think of the interplay of peripheral and central vision in terms of a "Cone of Vision," with the center of vision reacting more to changes in color and the peripheral being more sensitive to motion (**FIG 1.8**). This is very helpful when deciding what kinds of animations to use where in a design. If a user is looking directly at an element, a color fade or small movements might be enough to attract their attention during one of those saccades. But if a user isn't looking directly at something, we might need additional measures to get their attention.

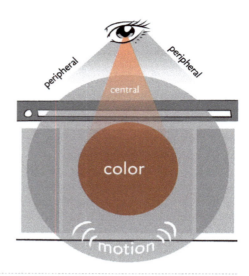

FIG 1.8: You can think of human sight as a Cone of Vision, with color sensitivity at the center and motion sensitivity toward the edges.

Change blindness and animacy

Change blindness is when a person's Cone of Vision doesn't pick up on a visual change. This happens offline all the time—you've probably returned to your desk or a familiar room before and didn't notice that an object was moved or taken away. But when change happens on a web page, we want users to be aware of it. One of the most effective ways to get change to register is to increase an item's *animacy*.

Animacy refers to a quality of "aliveness," usually tied to motion, shape, and other animatable properties. Studies show that the more alive something appears, the more likely it is to capture attention and thus break change blindness.

Change blindness is often a problem in cut interfaces with repeating patterns, like spreadsheets. It can take a few moments for users to reorient and see, *Oh yes, there's a new item right there.* But by animating an element, just a bit, we can harness the Cone of Vision to help users register the change.

FIG 1.9: Future generations will not remember these ads that wiggled and shook and sometimes even blared sounds at honest citizens of the Internet. (Watch the accompanying video.)

But animacy can be overdone. Cut interfaces are mentally taxing, as we've seen, because reorienting and puzzling out *What just happened?* are microdistractions. But high-motion animation can also be mentally taxing: users' brains work overtime to separate signal from noise. Remember back when banner ads blinked and shook and screamed at users to get them to click (**FIG 1.9**)?

Much like New Yorkers don't notice the huge flashing LCD signs that advertise shows on Broadway, users quickly become blind to unimportant change. To brains, high-animacy advertisements become nothing more than the wind rustling leaves.

In short, be considerate in your use of animacy. Respect the Cone of Vision.

DESIGNING WITH ANIMATION ISN'T ROCKET SCIENCE! (BUT IT IS NEUROSCIENCE.)

I've only introduced a small and vastly oversimplified sliver of the rich and deep bounty that neuroscience and cognitive psychology have to offer the field of web design. These are fascinating fields and a joy to study. Scientists are discovering new things about how the brain works *every day*. With better science we can build better things for a brighter tomorrow. If you want to learn more about how the human mind perceives the world around it, check out the Resources section.

That said, if you're feeling a little intimidated by all this "hijacking the human visual system for your own purposes" stuff, I've put together some starting points that are sure to apply to most any site or web app you find yourself working on. In the next chapter, we'll distill UI animation into five distinct categories and see when and how to apply them. Armed with the knowledge of how animation works with the human brain, you'll be even better able to decide when and where to use these types of animations for your users' benefit.

PATTERNS AND PURPOSE

SO WE CAN USE ANIMATIONS to tap into users' visual systems and give them a cognitive speed boost, terrific! But before animating every element of our designs, we must learn when and how to use this new tool: with great power comes great responsibility, and so forth. And as animation must vie with many other concerns for development and design time, it makes sense to spend our resources where they'll go the farthest.

This chapter sets you up with some core animation patterns and shows you how animation applies to a greater system. Then you'll learn how to spot cognitive bottlenecks and low-hanging fruit, maximizing the impact of the animations you do invest in.

COMMON ANIMATION PATTERNS

If you've looked at as many examples of animation on the web and in app interfaces as I have, certain patterns start to emerge. These patterns are helpful for identifying and succinctly verbalizing the purpose of an animation to others. Here are the categories I've found myself using the most:

- *Transitions* take users from place to place in the information space, or transition them out of one task into another. These tend to have massive impacts on the content on the page, replacing large portions of information.
- *Supplements* bring information on or off the page, but don't change the user's "location" or task. They generally add or update bits of additional content on the page.
- *Feedback* indicates causation between two or more events, often used to connect a user's interaction with the interface's reaction.
- *Demonstrations* explain how something works or expose its details by showing instead of telling.
- *Decorations* do not convey new information and are purely aesthetic.

Let's have a look at each of them and see how they impact the user's experience.

Transitions

The web was originally designed as a series of linked documents. Clicking on a link caused the browser to wipe the screen, often causing a telltale flash of white, before painting the next page from scratch. While this made sense in the context of linked text-based documents, it makes less sense in an era where pages share many rich design elements and belong to the same domain. Not only is it wasteful of the browser's resources to be recreating the same page layout over and over, but it also increases users' cognitive load when they have to reorient and reevaluate the page's content.

Animation, specifically motion, can facilitate the user's orientation in an information space by offloading that effort to the brain's visual cortex. Using a transition between changes in task flow or locations in information architecture ideally reinforces where the user has been, where they are going, and where they are now in one fell swoop.

For example, on Nike's SB Dunk page, when a user clicks a navigation arrow, the current sneaker moves out of the way while the next sneaker moves in from the opposite direction (**FIG 2.1**). These transitions clearly show the user how they are navigating along a linear continuum of sneakers, helping them keep track of their place and reinforcing the spatial model of perusing a real-world row of sneakers.

On another shoes site, fluevog.com, transitions move the user from task to task (**FIG 2.2**). After a user starts typing in the search field, the results are animated on top of a darker backdrop. This transitions the user from the browsing context to refining their search results, streamlining their focus while also reassuring them that they can get back to browsing without much effort.

When a user clicks one of the side arrows...

...the next sneaker slides in from the corresponding direction to show progression through the sneakers and reinforce their spatial locations.

FIG 2.1: On this Nike page, transitions are used to navigate forwards and backwards along a linear continuum of sneakers. (Watch the accompanying video.)

When a user clicks on the search icon...

...the search bar slides out of hiding, pushing the nav bar down from the top, its input field already in focus.

When the user starts typing, the search results overlay fades in to help them focus on live results.

FIG 2.2: On Fluevog's website, transitions move users from the browsing context to the searching context. (Watch the accompanying video.)

Supplements

While transitions move the user *from* state to state, supplemental animations bring ancillary information *to* the user. Think of times when information complementary to the main content of the page appears or disappears in view: alerts, dropdowns, and tooltips are all good candidates for a supplemental animation on entry and exit.

Remember that these animations need to respect the user's Cone of Vision: will they be looking directly at a tooltip appearing next to their cursor, or will their attention need to be directed to an alert on the side of their tablet?

a

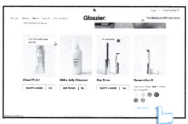

When a user clicks the Add to Bag button...

b

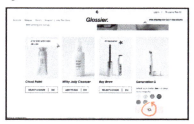

...the button gets a spinning loading icon to let the user know that the server is handling their request...

c

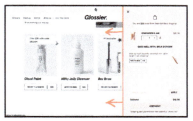

...when the request is done, the shopping cart sidebar slides out over the page...

d

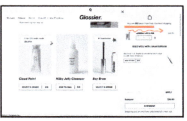

...then the free shipping meter animates to attract the user's attention to how much more they need to spend.

FIG 2.3: Glossier.com uses supplemental animation to show and hide the user's shopping cart, keeping them in the shopping context longer without forcing them into the purchasing context. (Watch the accompanying video.)

When a user adds a product to their shopping cart on glossier. com, rather than taking them to a whole new shopping cart page, the site merely updates the user as to their cart's contents by popping it out as a sidebar (**FIG 2.3C**). While a transition would snap the user out of browsing mode, this supplemental animation lets the user dismiss the shopping cart and continue shopping.

The shopping cart sidebar uses an additional supplemental animation to quickly and subtly attract the user's eye: a progress meter gradually fills to show how much the user needs to spend to get free shipping (**FIG 2.3D**).

This shopping cart process has a third animation pattern going on: the Add to Bag button gains a spinning icon when clicked, which gives the user feedback as to its loading state (**FIG 2.3B**). Speaking of feedback...

Feedback

Animation can give users direct feedback about their interactions. A depressed button, a swiping gesture—both link a human action to an interface's reaction. Or the flip side: a loading spinner on a page indicates that we're waiting on the computer. Without visual feedback, people are left wondering if they actually clicked that "pay now" button, or if the page is really loading after all.

On the Monterey Bay Aquarium's site, hovering over a button causes its color to fade from red to blue, indicating that the element is interactive and ready to react to user input (**FIG 2.4**). Button hovers are classic examples for this kind of animation,

a

When a user hovers over a button...

b

...the button's color changes to indicate the element is interactive.

FIG 2.4: On the Monterey Bay Aquarium's site, hovering on a button triggers an animation that gives the user feedback that the element is interactive. (Watch the accompanying video.)

a

b

c

When a user visits the site, a loading bar progresses across the top of the page to show how much longer till load.

When the page has fully loaded, the logo writes itself to indicate the wait is over and attract the user's attention to the middle of

...before the background fades in.

FIG 2.5: Design studio Animal uses a progress to let users know how much of the page has loaded, and an animated logo to indicate when it's fully loaded. (Watch the accompanying video.)

partly because the gain of giving users visual feedback on buttons is so measurable and important to business.

Design studio Animal's site uses a bar of color across the top of the page as well as an animated version of their logo to indicate the page's loading and loaded states *while* providing interest and reinforcing their "wild" branding (**FIG 2.5**).

Demonstrations

Demonstrations are my personal favorite use of animation. They can be both entertaining *and* insightful. These animations put information into perspective, show what's happening, or how something works. This makes demonstrative animations perfect partners for infographics. One thing all demonstrative animations do is tell a story, as you'll see.

"Processing…" pages are an opportunity to explain what's happening to users while they wait. TurboTax makes good use of these processing pages (**FIG 2.6**). After users submit their US tax forms, it banishes any remaining anxiety by showing them where their information is headed and what they can expect— all while reinforcing their brand's friendliness and accessibility. (It also helps that the animation distracts users from a rather lengthy page load with something visually engaging!)

a

When the user submits their taxes by clicking the "transmit" button...

b

...the form fades to white and then the office scene fades in and slides down...

c

...then an envelope representing the users taxes pops into view.

d

The envelope opens as, within the circle, files begin to fall into it...

e

...and when full, the envelope closes to show that their tax information has been gathered.

f

Then the envelop moves up and down as clouds whisk by within the circle, giving a feeling of transmission through the sky.

g

The envelope comes to rest and a checkmark pops up to show that its contents have been received

h

Then the envelope scoots out of the circle...

i

...and the whole scene simultaneously fades out while sliding up while the circle shrinks

FIG 2.6: TurboTax both informs their users and masks long page loads by demonstrating what's going on after the user submits their US tax forms. (Watch the accompanying video.)

Coin famously uses demonstrative animations to explain their consolidation card's value proposition to curious visitors as they scroll through the site (**FIG 2.7**)—no need to press play

a

When a user visits the site, they're presented with an autoplaying video demonstrating the value proposition.

b

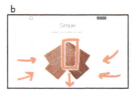

As the user scrolls, they see visual demonstrations of the same proposition, starting with many cards merging into one...

c

...then the one card slides underneath the next section.

d

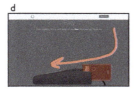

As the user continues to scroll, the card follows and swipes the card reader...

e

...then comes to rest next to the iPhone before flicking away casually to

f

At the very bottom of the page, the card slides up as if saying it was there for us all

FIG 2.7: As visitors scroll through Coin's site, the company's value proposition plays out in front of them. (Watch the accompanying video.)

and sit through a video ad or wade through paragraphs of expository content. This page is the very essence of "show, don't tell."

Decorations

It's not hard to mistake decorative animations for demonstrative animations. But there is a key difference: where demonstrations bring new information into the system, decorative animations do not. They are the fats and sugars of the animation food pyramid: they make great flavor enhancers, but moderation is key.

The best way to spot a purely decorative animation is to ask, "What can a user learn from this animation? Does this guide them or show them something they wouldn't know

a

On page load, the door is closed.

b

Then the spotlight shines down as the bright patch expands...

c

...then the door opens to reveal a symbol representing women.

HOLD for a beat.

d

She rises up slightly as suddenly a hole opens up beneath her!

e

She falls down the hole.

f

Then the door swings closed as the spotlight recedes.

g

The hole shrinks to nothing.

h

And we're back at the first frame like nothing happened. Like she was never there.

FIG 2.8: Revisionist History's site uses decorative animations to add visual interest to non-visual media. (Watch the accompanying video.)

otherwise?" If the answer is no, you might have a decorative animation on your hands.

Even though they get a bad rap, decorative animations can help turn the ordinary into the extraordinary. Revisionist History's site uses decorative animations judiciously to bring flat illustrations to life. The animations add just enough interest

a

Users at first see a blank, green screen.

b

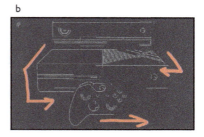

Promptly the console draws itself in.

c

When the illustration is complete, its buttons press...

d

...then the illustration shrinks upward while the article rises to meet it.

FIG 2.9: Polygon uses decorative animations as a showstopping feature to stand out from the competition. (Watch the accompanying video.)

to allow for the visual content on the page to be more austere, letting users focus on the podcast (**FIG 2.8**).

Polygon.com epically used animated illustrations to create centerpieces for a series of console reviews. These decorative animations may not have added new information, but they crucially reinforced the Polygon brand. They also helped each console review stand out from the competition, which at the time sported indistinguishable photographs of the same devices.

PURPOSE

Once we've started noticing patterns, it's easier to talk about purpose. All of these patterns (with the exception of maybe the decorative ones) do something important: they supply context in a context-poor environment.

The world around us is alive with information in the form of noises, smells, and movements, and it responds when we interact with it. The web is rich with information, but it's not inherently rich with context and feedback. Animation can and should help with that, from providing feedback about the status of your tax return submission to attracting your attention to a crucial update. That is animation's true purpose: to add context.

An easy way to check if an animation provides context is to use your words to describe what benefit or new information it supplies. From the Nike example (**FIG 2.1**), we could say, "The sneakers move forward or backward to show the user where they are in a linear list of shoes, and what direction they are moving in along that list."

The more easily we can describe how an animation enriches the information on the page, the more context it likely provides. And the more context an animation provides, the more justified we are in supplying it. Context-rich animations have purpose and real meaning on the page, as opposed to existing solely to "delight."

Thinking about animation early

To make sure that our animations are purposeful, it pays to starting thinking about them as early as possible in a project. When web projects are in the planning stages, it's important to have conversations about animation with as many stakeholders as possible, from development to design and UX. Look for opportunities to bring animation into the discussion.

- **Information architecture and navigation structure** can be augmented with motion design. How can you reinforce a user's location in the site's data space? How can you convey their transition from location to location within that space, or their progression through tasks?

- **Interaction design** opens up when animation comes to the table. Static interfaces tend to require much more wording to explain relationships that animation can visually demonstrate. What interactions are you overexplaining?
- **Branding** can be reinforced by animations—both overtly with decorative animations, and discreetly with easing and animation language (more on those in the next chapter). What kind of emotions should your brand evoke, and how can animation reinforce them?

We'll talk more about generating buy-in and collaborating in a little bit, but for now, know that the more folks are listening at the start, the more your animations are likely to make it into the final product.

Spotting cognitive bottlenecks

Not all of us are so fortunate as to be at the start of a new project when it comes time to implement animations. When tasked with adding animations to an existing project, we run the risk of only implementing "delighters"—decorative animations that reinforce branding or live up to stakeholder expectations, but don't necessarily improve cognitive flow for users.

Don't give up hope: seize this opportunity! The cut interface of most websites gives off plenty of "cognitive bottleneck smells" that we can home in on and mitigate with animations:

- **Flashes of white** happen when a new page is loaded and painted into the browser window. Why replace the whole page when you can change and animate just the parts that matter? If the new content is different from the old in purpose or location, consider using a transition to take the user there. If the design of the pages is identical and its content the same, a supplemental animation might be just the trick to bring the changes into play.
- **Content insertion or removal** is a prime candidate for animation: tooltips, menus, dialogs, sequenced information.

- **Wordy descriptions** can indicate something being told instead of shown. Can a demonstration do it better?
- **Videos**, in the same vein, can be overkill for demonstrations in some cases and require user interaction to stop or start. Can an animated demonstration convey the same information passively and with fewer megabytes?

Prioritization

In his book *Creativity, Inc.,* Pixar's Ed Catmull mentions a phenomenon their producers have dubbed "the beautifully shaded penny." This refers to how creative folks tend to pour a lot of energy into a feature that is actually quite small in the greater scheme of the project. Katherine Sarafian, a Pixar producer, called it "the equivalent of a penny on a nightstand that you'll never see." For instance, a scene in *Monsters, Inc.* included a stand of alphabetized CDs—each one with a carefully designed cover—but in the actual film, we only see three of them.

It's easy for me, as an animation wonk, to walk in on a project and see all the opportunities to animate. But animation has to jostle with many other features for developer time—from performance to typography—and resources are not limitless. So we have to prioritize to make sure we get the most impactful animations into the project while leaving some of the nice-to-haves for another day.

Just because an animation makes something look nicer doesn't mean it's worth the effort to implement from a development standpoint. Consider whether or not it's adding information back into the system. Is it a working animation or an entertaining animation? We can weigh it and find out!

First, find out what patterns the animation falls into. If something is both a transition and a demonstration, that's a double-whammy: it's providing *even more* valuable context.

Then, to help quantify that context, ask the following questions:

- Does it show the user where information came from or went to?
- Does it indicate progress?
- Does it move the user through an information space?
- Does it reinforce physics or branding?
- Does it explain something faster than words or a video could?

The more boxes an animation ticks and patterns it fulfills, the more likely it is to provide a net gain for your users, and the more justifiable it becomes. This is how you know it's not just a nice-to-have.

But not all justifiable animations are feasible within the scope of a project. You may lack resources to implement a new framework to allow page transitions, for instance. To help visualize which animations to focus on, I create a graph with "ease of implementation" on the X-axis (ranging from easy to implement to difficult) and "justification" on the Y-axis (ranging from nice-to-have to necessary), and plot the animation features on it accordingly (**FIG 2.10**). Every animation you'd like to use will rank somewhere on this chart.

Does the animation tie into another priority, like performance or a highly anticipated new feature? When an animation ties in with another effort, it's more likely to involve more parties and resources may be more or less available because of that. I give these kinds of efforts a bigger size on the graph to visually indicate the weight of their undertaking.

Next, I draw a cross over the graph (I know, it's sad to mar such a beautiful graph, but this is the important part) (**FIG 2.11**). Usually we end up with the following categories of importance:

- **Low-hanging fruit** represents big wins at low cost. There are few good reasons to delay working on these, and they should be moved to the top of the priority heap across the board. Prioritizing them will net you big wins.
- **Long-term investments** represent animations that will help people a lot, but require more effort to execute. To make sure the result is what you expect, run some prototypes by users and gauge their reactions. The animation may not be

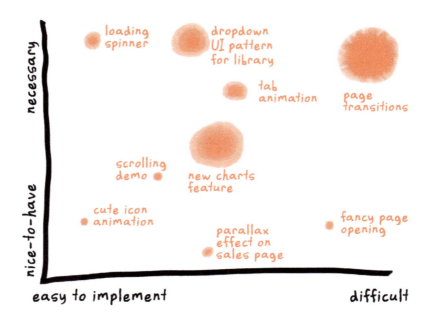

necessary

nice-to-have

loading spinner

dropdown UI pattern for library

tab animation

page transitions

scrolling demo

new charts feature

cute icon animation

parallax effect on sales page

fancy page opening

easy to implement

difficult

FIG 2.10: Plot your potential animations on the chart according to how necessary and difficult to implement they are.

as important as thought, or if it is, use the results of the test to help justify prioritizing the time for it in the future. Try not to leave long-term investments in the icebox for too long, though! Ignore them, and your project won't be all it can be.

· **Pet projects** are great to keep around for slow days (they happen) and to hand out to new recruits as a special challenge. (Who wouldn't jump at the chance to animate a "favorite" icon on their first day?)

· **Hopeless causes** are both unnecessary *and* difficult to implement. Just accept that you will never have the time or the justification to work on them. If someone else magically gets them done, have a long talk with them. Maybe they

Necessary / nice-to-have / easy to implement / difficult

low hanging fruit

loading spinner

dropdown UI pattern for library

longterm investments

animation page transitions

scrolling demo

new charts feature

pet projects

cute icon animation

parallax effect on sales page

YOU WILL NEVER GET TO THESE

fancy page loading

FIG 2.11: Divide your chart into quadrants to help identify your priorities.

know a technique worth learning—or they might need their priorities adjusted.

Larger dots that touch more teams will need to be brought up earlier in a project. When it comes to animation, the more planning and integration time people have, the more likely the animation is to make it into the feature. Think of these bigger dots as opportunities to collaborate across teams and build something everyone is proud of.

USEFUL AND NECESSARY, THEN BEAUTIFUL

The Shaker people have a design philosophy that suffuses their craftsmanship: "Don't make something unless it is both necessary and useful; but if it is both necessary and useful, don't hesitate to make it beautiful."

We have a tendency to talk about animations as "beautiful" or "delightful," but delight alone is not a reason to use an animation. When crafting for delight, we risk creating a purely decorative animation that will wear on users' nerves after the fiftieth viewing. Animation is not in and of itself delightful. But when used considerately with all the other pieces in the system—the typography, the interface, the voice and tone of the site, the speed of content delivery—the *whole* experience becomes delightful.

Now you should be able to distinguish useful, necessary, and even beautiful animations from one another, and be able to spot opportunities to use them. But great animation ideas must be conveyed across great teams. And to do that, we need a technical vocabulary developers understand. In the next chapter we're going to focus on the terminology of web animations and how their different components work together.

3

ANATOMY OF A WEB ANIMATION

I ONCE HAD A PROJECT where a designer gave me an animated GIF to recreate in CSS. (Please, please do *not* send developers animated GIFs and no guidelines to work from at 4:30pm. It's a form of cruelty, I'm certain.) I stayed up all night remaking it in CSS until it looked like a perfect replica—to *my* eyes. However, when the designer came back in the next morning, the first thing they noticed was that I hadn't translated an almost imperceptible bounce!

If only they had provided me with a little extra information, I would have been able to recreate that GIF perfectly and in much less time. To do that, I would have needed to know three things about the animation:

- *Easing*: The rate at which the visual changes occur—for instance, going from slow to fast.
- *Duration*: How long the animation should last, often in fractions of a second.
- *Properties*: What visual aspects you want to change, like width or color.

Let's have a closer look at these three comrades.

EASING

Easing describes the rate at which something changes over a period time. When applied to motion, easing can describe an element's acceleration or deceleration. The term has its roots in traditional studio animation, where it was called "cushioning" or even "slowing."

In CSS, easings are called *timing functions* and are described in a few ways. Every browser understands the default CSS timing function keywords:

- `ease-in` (acceleration)
- `ease-out` (deceleration)
- `ease-in-out` (speed up then slow down)
- `linear` (constant rate of change)

Each of these easings works best in different situations:

- Acceleration is good for system-initiated animations, like a pop-up asking users to sign up for a newsletter. If this unannounced animation starts slowly, it's less likely to startle users, even if it takes the same amount of time as an animation with an ease-in.
- Deceleration starts quickly and gives a UI a snappy, responsive feeling. It's great for user-initiated interactions, like button clicks and page transitions.
- Speeding up then slowing down is useful for interaction models when moving an element toward another.
- A constant rate of change works best for fades and color changes, which can look jarring with a steep curve.
- Bounces can add extra animacy to draw attention to elements or to add an air of "fun" to the brand.

These easing values look and feel the same from browser to browser, site to site. But if you want your animation to stand out, to feel unique to your site, you'll want custom easings. CSS has a special format for customizing easing: the *cubic Bézier curve.*

Cubic Béziers are a formula used to mathematically describe a rate of change. When plotted on a graph, a cubic Bézier will form a curve with steepness indicating a quicker rate of change. This formula can be shared in CSS by putting the curve's coordinates into the `cubic-bezier(w, x, y, z)` timing function. Because of its flexibility, this formula also lets us create single and double bounces. Even CSS's default timing functions can be described as cubic Bézier curves (**FIG 3.1**)!

Cubic-bezier.com is a great tool that lets you tug and pull the handles of the curve in real time, updating the formula while you watch. Both Chrome and Firefox have similar tools, which I highly recommend trying out. Playing with tools like these is a fun way to get a feel for the way easings work.

But you might prefer starting with the tried and true formulae at easings.net. These have been used in interaction design for years. Is your brand gentle and elegant like a Sine curve, or fast-paced and bursting with energy like the steeper Expo? Give

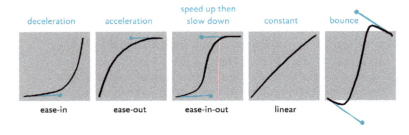

FIG 3.1: CSS's default easings described as `cubic-bezier()` curves.

them all a spin, and copy and paste the formulae for the ones that feel the most like your brand.

Speaking of branding, it's best to keep animations looking uniform throughout your site's experience. The best way to do that is to create a collection of harmonious easings for reuse. It's helpful to keep them all in a chart detailing their purpose, their cubic Bézier formula or CSS keyword, and where said formula came from (**FIG 3.2**).

PURPOSE	ORIGIN	CSS TIMING FUNCTION
Acceleration	EaseInCubic from easings.net	`cubic-bezier (0.55, 0.055, 0.675, 0.19)`
Deceleration	EaseOutCubic from easings.net	`cubic-bezier (0.215, 0.61, 0.355, 1)`
Ease-in-out	EaseInOutCubic from easings.net	`cubic-bezier (0.645, 0.045, 0.355, 1)`
Subtle curve	Browser default keyword	`linear`
Bounce	Custom-made at cubic-bezier.com	`cubic-bezier (.61,-0.23,.36,1.35)`

FIG 3.2: An easings chart can tamp down on proliferating easing usage and provide a unified feel for your site's animations.

DURATION

Animation is change over time. To create any animation, it helps to know its duration. While easings tell us the rate of change, the duration tells us how long the animation lasts. But how long *should* an animation last? We can make some inferences.

Perhaps you're familiar with Jakob Nielsen's "Three Important Time Limits" post from 1993? In it, Nielsen referenced a 1968 study that measured human reactions to computer response times. The results of the study showed that:

- Response times of 100 milliseconds or less felt instantaneous.
- Response times of up to 1 second still felt connected.
- After 10 seconds, users began to feel disconnected.

These durations are referenced by many UX community members to this day for gauging human-computer interactions. But remember that this research was done in 1968, and it was already almost three decades old when Nielsen wrote about it.

People use computers very differently from how they did in the late 1960s, and it appears their patience is running out. In 2009, Google ran experiments where they slowed down their search results pages by 100 to 400 milliseconds. The slower response times had a measurable impact on the number of searches per user. Even weeks later, users from the slowed pages were not searching as much. Another Google study from 2016 indicates that 53% of mobile site visits are abandoned if they take longer than three seconds to load. Previous research *really* should be revisited in this new era of touchscreens and beefy graphics cards.

Fortunately, we have some other resources to draw from, and the time units involved are all under one second long. While CSS can accept both seconds and milliseconds, JavaScript only takes millisecond values. Thus it makes sense to think of and document our animation durations in terms of milliseconds first.

The average time it takes people to react to visual change is about 215 ms. Thus, it makes sense that 200-300 ms is a recurring sweet spot among game and interaction developers. Durations in this range tend to be the workhorses in an interface.

The Model Human Processor (a system used to quantify human computer interactions) clocks the time it takes a user's eye to move at between 70 and 700 ms. It follows that animations in the center of the user's Cone of Vision do better with shorter durations (closer to the 70-200 ms spectrum) because the eye has less distance to travel. Animations on the edge of the Cone of Vision benefit from additional time for the user to move their eye, over in the 300-700 ms spectrum.

If something is moving across a screen, it will need more time than something providing immediate feedback, like a color change on hover. The eye is quite sensitive to color changes when it's looking directly at the animation. For that reason, I've found that color and opacity changes under the user's finger or cursor can feel slow if they take more than 100 ms. But if you're moving something across the page, 100 ms is too fast, and going over 300 ms may be necessary. It's important to try out various durations with real users to find the "Goldilocks duration" that feels "just right" for your use case.

Production speed

Studio animators working tirelessly on scenes week after week get pulled into a warped sense of time and space where their animation's playback seems faster than it really is. This is why animators have a saying: "Whatever your pre-production duration is, halve it. Then halve it again!"

This happens to us on the web, too. When preparing an animation, we also tend to perceive it as running faster than it really is. It's not uncommon to slash a production animation's duration to 25% of its development length. Just be sure that you're still giving the animation enough time to run if the user blinks or the animation doesn't render perfectly smoothly. The developer tools in both Chrome and Firefox can help you run animations faster or slower for debugging (**FIG 3.3**).

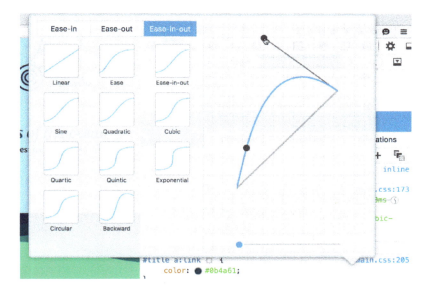

FIG 3.3: Firefox's developer tools offer presets as well as customization options for cubic Bézier curves. Dragging the handles on the curve changes the playback rate of the animation, with steeper segments running faster than more gradual slopes. (Watch the accompanying video.)

Timing scales

Just as with easings, durations can be arranged into reusable sets, with different durations for color changes, localized reactions like button presses, and large movements. But we don't have to select numbers out of thin air; we can use timing scales. The concept is similar to modular scales in typography: all values are related, and if you combine them with a vertical rhythm, a piece exhibits overall harmony.

Amy Lee, prototyper at Salesforce by day and musician by night, first introduced me to the concept of reusable and interlocking timing values on Salesforce's Lightning Design System.

KEYWORD	DURATION IN MILLISECONDS	USE
Immediate	100 ms	For fades and color-based animations
Fast	300 ms	For interacting with elements that need to feel responsive and peppy
Slower	400 ms	For moving elements on the page
Deliberate	700 ms	For large movements across the screen or self-contained demonstrations

FIG 3.4: This timing scale is inspired by the Fibonacci sequence: 100 + 300 = 400, 300 + 400 = 700. Referring to a chart like this will, once again, help standardize animations across a site.

> *[It] is about an agreed-upon synchronization of animation choreography. Imagine how an orchestra might play together. Without a common timing system, each player would drift through the score at their own rate. However, if we agree that a quarter note is 400ms long, then we all can play together at a peppy tempo of 150 beats per minute.*

You can generate a timing scale the same way you generate a typographic scale. Salesforce's Lightning Design System uses timing scales to let developers tokenize their timing values. It's easy to line overlapping animations up to end at the same time with a system like this (FIG 3.4).

PROPERTIES

Properties describe *what* is changing over time. Color and opacity changes convey fades. Changes in location convey motion. Changes in scale or shape convey deformation and transformation.

Having a record of what CSS properties change is very helpful to developers—and for long-term documentation. When we record all this information in storyboards (we'll get to those in the next chapter), it leaves a clear blueprint for others to follow tomorrow.

Performance

Not all properties are as easy to animate for different browsers. Many of them trigger costly layout and painting operations in the browser, which on an overworked or underpowered device can cause an animation to drop a few frames—aka stuttering, or what studio animators refer to as "juttering" or becoming "janky." Jank breaks the illusion of life, so it's important to stick to performant properties. Properties like `opacity` and `transform` (which *transforms* scale, position, rotation) are currently pretty safe bets. Many browsers optimize their rendering pipeline to process `opacity` and `transform` animations on the computer's GPU.

But there will be times when we want to animate less performant things like `width` or `borders`. Browsers are working hard to improve their animation performance, so while it's great to try to stick to `transform` and `opacity`, don't be afraid to push boundaries where it has negligible impact on the animation's overall performance.

John Lasseter of Pixar said, "The art challenges the technology, and the technology inspires the art." It's true that what we do with animation today impacts what browser vendors build for tomorrow. It's a beautiful push and pull of needs.

PUTTING IT ALL TOGETHER

Now that we have all the building blocks required to describe and document an animation, we'll dive into how to turn animations into deliverables for your teams. We'll meet some old tools from studio animation and learn how to rally support for an animation agenda.

COMMUNICATING
ANIMATION

ANIMATION SITS AT THE INTERSECTION of UX, development, and design. This means it can bring teams together—or drive them apart! Communication issues and inadequate deliverable documentation can make it hard for teams to design and build out animations quickly, leaving things like motion design and gestures at the bottom of the pile for implementation. Lack of respect and deference to one another can lead to deprioritization, and exclusionary gatekeeping can keep animation from being fully embraced across an organization.

Fortunately, animation can be nestled into our existing design and development processes and documentation. We have been using things like UI pattern libraries to document microinteractions and style guides to contain our typography and color palettes. With a systematic approach, we can bring animations to heel as well.

This chapter is all about communicating your animation patterns across teams, and getting everyone on board the "animation train."

CRAFTING AN ANIMATION LANGUAGE

The key to any interaction model is consistency. When I was new to web animation, I wanted to animate all the things. UI animation was new and exciting and looked so polished! But when I looked at all my animations working on the same site, they weren't working together. Was I going to get a modal fading in or sliding in? Were all the icons animated, or just the ones I had time to get to and thought were clever? Was every page going to transition in, or just this set over here?

UI animation works best when it conforms to predetermined sets of rules. And if you're working on a large project with a long-term growth plan, you'll want to use animations that can be adapted to multiple uses while maintaining cohesion and consistency. This is where animation language comes in.

We can combine the three components of animation that we discussed in Chapter 3—easing, duration, and properties—to create microanimations with descriptive names like "pop," "fade," and "slide." A microanimation can be used as part of a

FIG 4.1: Salesforce provides a rich vocabulary of predefined microanimations for developers to use and combine into new patterns. (Watch the accompanying video.)

greater design pattern, or combined with other microanimations to create macroanimations—for instance, a modal that fades onto the screen then pops to grab user attention. We might then label that combined animation as an "alert," and use it over and over again.

Many of these microanimation names start as friendly onomatopoeias around a meeting room table: swoosh, zoom, plonk, boom. Something I've noticed at many companies around the world is that participants will hold a sound longer to indicate extended duration: "Can you make it more like *voooooosh* and less like *voosh*?" It makes sense to "pave the cowpaths" and adopt the words your company is using already.

When codified, these microanimations can form animation vocabularies that yield huge benefits when it comes time to document visual deliverables with text. Salesforce's Lightning Design System provides developers with a host of these microanimations to compose whatever custom designs or interfaces its users create. In this way, Salesforce engenders brand compliance by providing easy-to-reach-for defaults (**FIG 4.1**).

Salesforce could have provided lengthier documentation explaining the choices their design team made, but the Lightning Design Team chose to lead by examples and easy, composable presets, providing a path of least resistance for developers who are probably more interested in getting a product out the door than learning the intricacies of UI animation that you are (and you are so awesome for it).

DOCUMENTING ANIMATION FOR DESIGN SYSTEMS

There are two reasons to document design decisions:

1. To create deliverables for developers to implement.
2. To create guidelines for designers and developers to follow in the future.

Nowhere is this more important than with animation. Animation cannot be conveyed in a single screenshot. And while it can be demonstrated in a GIF or a video, developers have to pick apart those formats with more or less fidelity. None of these alone are good formats for communicating animation deliverables in the present or future. They cannot be passed to an external agency as one would a branding bible or style guide. They cannot be referenced when creating choreographed systems that look and feel the same across a user's journey.

To build scalable, maintainable, integrated designs, we need to document not just the anatomy of their animations (as seen in Chapter 3), but also how those animations should be choreographed in the context of user interaction. Lucky for us, we have a couple of tools that can help.

Storyboards

In 1933, Disney Studios crafted the world's first storyboards in preparation for working on the world's first feature-length animated film, *Snow White and the Seven Dwarfs*. The storyboards reduced time spent on poorly planned shots, and helped directors and writers visualize the final story and edit it on the fly, taking studio animation from a waterfall workflow to an agile one. Storyboards made *Snow White* possible, and the Hollywood directors who had mocked Disney's dream of an animated movie soon found themselves adopting storyboards for their own projects.

These days, storyboards are used not only in cinema but also in game design, interaction development, and—you guessed it—even in web design. Storyboards are useful because they put words, even values, next to snapshots of an animation.

Storyboards can help explicitly state how an interaction is expected to be implemented. They can reduce the load on developers and are a great place to document *why* a decision was made (FIG 4.2).

I like to make my initial storyboards the old-fashioned way: with index cards and corkboards or Post-Its and sketchbooks. But even I use an officious, cleaned-up template (PDF) for client deliverables and archival purposes. For those with a completely digital workflow, boords.com provides a promising solution, with PDF exports and a simplified interface (compared to cinematic storyboarding software!).

Storyboards are great for archiving design decisions and setting standards, but they fall short in a few ways. You can't demonstrate or test an animation's look and feel with them, and they are clunky to integrate with existing online design guidelines. But, as far as quantifying what changes when, tried and true storyboards can't be beat.

a

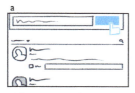

b

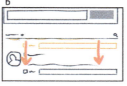

c

When a user adds a new friend by clicking the button...

...the new friend slides down from the top of the list over 200ms with an ease-in...

...displacing the friends below, drawing attention to where the new friend can be found while confirming that the friend was

FIG 4.2: The second frame describes the animation's duration and easing, and the third frame explains what benefit the animation provides. (Watch the accompanying video.)

Animatics

Where storyboards excel at providing deliverable values and inline reasoning, they fall short at conveying an animation's "mouthfeel." Stakeholders are unlikely to be satisfied with a presentation of a storyboard. If a picture is worth a thousand words, then an animatic must be worth a thousand meetings.

Once again, studio animation provides a solution in the form of *animatics*: videos of the storyboard panels set to an audio track with the actors reading their lines and the soundtrack playing. Animatics can be shown to a test audience to see how they respond to a plot twist, or presented to investors as proof of progress.

For creating animatics, Adobe After Effects is the current software of choice in the motion design industry. Web designers may be more accustomed to creating animatic-like demos in Keynote, which can be clicked through in meetings or recorded with screencasting software like Quicktime or Camtasia. And some visual prototyping tools, like Principle, export to video achieving two things at once. You can also make animatics as small videos or GIFs. If you're a paper prototyper, you can even use a stop-motion app on your phone to record an animatic (**FIG 4.3**)!

FIG 4.3: Animatics come in all shapes and forms, from super-polished designs made in After Effects to stop-motion films. I made this one with Post-Its and a stop-motion app on my phone. (Watch the accompanying video.)

Prototypes

Animatics can provide a visual "aha!" moment for stakeholders, but they are impossible to test in the field. Something that sounds good in theory and looks good on a big screen in a meeting room can still frustrate users in practice. Prototypes give us the chance to observe real people doing real things with our animations.

There are two approaches to prototypes: prototyping frameworks that require a knowledge of HTML and CSS, and prototyping software that offers a visual interface to work with. Developers tend to prefer the former, often leaning on frameworks like Framer, while many designers prefer the latter in the form of software like InVision.

Both approaches require team members to invest time in learning a new system, thus increasing the commitment factor. Essentially, prototyping involves making the site twice: once as a working mockup and then again as product-ready code. While large companies can afford entire prototyping teams and reap the benefits of "measure twice, cut once," this is prohibitive for many small businesses and agencies. But for those who can afford it, it's a solid approach to designing with animation.

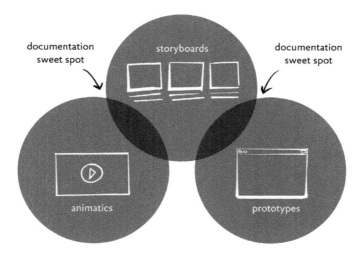

FIG 4.4: The best approach to documentation is to couple verbal and visual descriptions together.

Verbal and visual documentation

Prototypes, unlike storyboards, are terrible for documentation: only code-savvy team members can read them, and the files must be organized and sometimes compiled or served before inspection. On the other hand, animatics are terrible for developers to work from because they don't provide values for an animation's easing, duration, and properties. An external agency would struggle to deliver a fully branded experience riffing off a pile of non-production code or animated GIFs. And storyboards, while archival, convey nothing of motion in action.

So what do we do? The best approach to get both deliverables and archival information is to combine two of these approaches: coupling animatics with storyboards, or adding live microinteractions to design systems along with the values necessary to reproduce them (**FIG 4.4**). The former works great on smaller teams and projects on a shoestring budget, while the latter reinforces the authority of a larger enterprise.

GENERATING BUY-IN

Now we know how to share animations in formats that communicate their actions and the technical details required to recreate them. But as anyone who's tried to create a style guide alone has learned, "if you document it, they will come" is a fallacy. We need to get our teammates excited about animation!

Focus on the benefits

First you might be inclined to argue with numbers and facts. But this can be tricky. Understanding the inherent value of animation requires an understanding of how the human visual system works, something even renowned academics struggle with.

What's more, arguing for or defending animation can cause friction with some folks who don't like being challenged over seemingly unimportant "decoration." So why not skip combat mode altogether and talk benefits? If stakeholders collaborate, document, and codify their efforts together, their animations will pay off with:

- **Lighter code.** When animation is normalized, it's unlikely to be repeated in numerous permutations throughout a codebase.
- **Reliable interaction patterns.** Consistent interactions bolster user confidence and trust. Dropdowns that slide down alongside ones that fade in, for instance, make an interface feel shifty and unfinished.
- **Maintainability.** Reliable, repeatable, consolidated animations are easier to maintain than their fly-by-the-seat-of-their-pants counterparts.
- **On-brand interaction.** Animations can reflect the brand's voice and tone, reinforcing branding.
- **Shorter design and development time.** If animations don't need to be tooled from scratch for every bit of interaction, spinning up rich new experiences is that much faster.

Show, don't tell

There's one sure way to drive home how much difference animation makes: show it. As Robert Greene wrote in his Machiavellian book, *The 48 Laws of Power,* "It is much more powerful to get others to agree with you through your actions, without saying a word. Demonstrate, do not explicate." So often when animation is picked up for a project, it's because someone placed an animated version next to a static comp so stakeholders could see the difference for themselves.

From big companies like Google to small ad agencies, showing beats telling. Getting the animations out of your head and in front of the eyes of people who matter beats lobbying. Trust human intuition to convince a skeptical audience. The brain's GPU can't be denied.

Spread the love

An animation-friendly mindset must be cultivated and championed around the workplace. Someone has to keep it top of mind when it would be forgotten during prototyping. Someone has to keep an eye on the latest research and performance tricks. Why can't that person be you?

But be wary of falling into the trap of trying to own animation for your team or company. I've watched companies lose all momentum on bringing animation into their UI when the one person who internally evangelized motion design left. Setting yourself up as a lone gatekeeper is dangerous—not just for the company, but also for you. You could be seen as the obsessive animation wonk who thinks the world revolves around "silly decorative stuff." It's easy to ignore one person, but a group of allied experts is a force to be reckoned with. You'll have a better chance of getting animation on the table at the start of a project.

Look for collaborators outside your own department. If you're in design, a developer can help you prototype ideas or build out UI patterns. If you're in UX, a designer can help you make animatics that win over managers. And don't forget about accessibility, branding, and performance folks. Because animation touches so many disciplines, it has the magical power to bring people together who otherwise might never collaborate. Find these people and befriend them.

Animation as a team sport

Once again, think of yourself more as a gardener, not a gatekeeper. When working on animations, share your work with your teams. Let them get excited. Take their feedback. If they want to help document or prototype, no matter how briefly, let them touch the project and feel part ownership. When everyone feels like this is their baby, they're less likely to throw it out with the bath water.

WHEN A PLAN COMES TOGETHER

For animation to be a part of a balanced design, many different moving parts need to come together—literally! You must be attentive to details, consistent in your approach, and document every decision. But none of this matters if no one adopts these guidelines. Providing an animation vocabulary helps: it gives your partners useful, on-brand defaults to get started with. But more than anything, it's up to you to bring people together, which requires setting egos aside and solving problems greater than any of us can tackle alone.

BEST PRACTICES AND OTHER EDUCATED GUESSES

ANIMATION ON THE WEB is nothing new, but it's enjoying a comeback at a time when we care deeply about accessibility and usability. This is a good thing because it reminds us to put animation to work *for* our users, instead of just using it for our own entertainment and delight.

Unfortunately, past web animators from the Flash era didn't leave many best practices or guidelines for us to follow. We are new to using animation in this purposeful, respectful way. Not a month passes that I don't learn something new about how different people perceive motion and change, or how we can create even more useful animations.

As such, the following "best practices" are more like guidelines to follow and test while we uncover more and more about how animation works—and doesn't work—on the web.

NO ONE SHOULD NOTICE THE WAITSTAFF

There is nothing so satisfying as hearing a beta tester remark, "Oh, that's delightful!" upon seeing your first UI animations. However, this could be a red flag. It means that they have noticed an animation, and that means they are spending cognitive power on it—the exact opposite of what animations should do. There are some circumstances, such as demonstrative animations, where we want people to really notice the action. But for the majority of microinteractions, we don't want animations to distract users.

I like to think of animation as the waitstaff at a fancy restaurant. You come to eat and drink, and to have good conversation with your companions. A good server facilitates this. No sooner have you set your fork down than your dinner plate seemingly disappears and is replaced with a dessert dish. As Heather Daggett, senior experience design prototyper at Intuit who works regularly with animation, put it:

Users should only notice your animation if you need to attract their attention in that moment. Otherwise, micro-interactions and other transitions should be so seamless, users don't even notice that there is animation.

When testing with users, pay attention to when they notice animation and when they don't. We know we're reducing their cognitive load when they don't notice something.

CONSISTENCY IS KEY

I mentioned in the previous chapter that consistency is important to creating a unified experience for our users, and that extends to animations. Beyond just using the same easings across a site or adhering to an animation language, we want to make sure that animations behave consistently as well.

Every entrance needs an exit

When a piece of information animates onto the screen, it should also animate as it leaves the screen. Because of how HTML, CSS, and JavaScript are often used together, it is often easier to animate an element's entrance than its exit. As such, many alerts beautifully animate into view, only to cut back into the void as soon as the user dismisses them (**FIG 5.1**). This gives a UI an unfinished, unreliable feel.

To provide a user with a consistent experience, we must invest early and wisely in a system that waits for an exit animation to finish before removing an element or changing state.

a

When a user goes to point at a navigation menu item...

b

...the menu expands downward when hovered over...

c

...and stays expanded until the hover is moved...

d

...whereupon the menu disappears immediately from the page without animation.

FIG 5.1: Sights like this are unfortunately commonplace: on Duluth Trading Company's site, the dropdowns expand downward when users hover over their link. But when the mouse moves away, those submenus disappear. (Watch the accompanying video.)

Avoid FOULS

You may have heard of flashes of unstyled text, or FOUT, that happen when a page's fonts haven't loaded yet so it displays default system fonts. Perhaps you've also met its cousin, FOULS: Flashes of Unloaded/ing States. These are often glimpsed when first loading or leaving a page on sites rich with transitions and supplementary information: briefly there's a flash of a page with no content, possibly followed by a loading state, then a page with the loaded content. These can happen in any order,

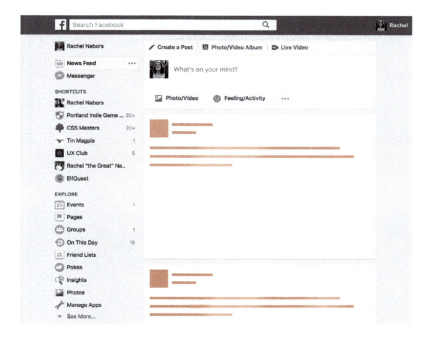

FIG 5.2: The "Facebook Shimmer" uses lightly animated or "shimmering" bars and blocks for placeholder content until the real content loads. (Watch the accompanying video.)

and when they do, they leave users wondering (again!), "What just happened?"

Loading states can mask empty pages bereft of content from users by providing an indication that the content is on its way. Ideally it flows like this:

1. A user lands on a page with no loaded content. But rather than showing an **unloaded** page...
2. ...the page starts in a **loading** state, showing indicators that content is coming and/or where it will be soon. (Facebook's "shimmer" pattern is a good example of this (**FIG 5.2**). Spinners in place of loading images are another example.)
3. Finally, the newly arrived content transitions to a **loaded** state.

When a user clicks on a link to another part of the site...

...the content fades out and slides up...

...but then the same content fades in and slides down, flashing an inappropriate loading state...

...before the new page with a very different design cuts into place.

FIG 5.3: This example of FOULS comes from a version of my own site, RachelNabors.com. So very embarrassing! (Watch the accompanying video.)

Loading states are very useful, but only if they actually hide the unloaded content from detection. We must ensure that users always see loaded states in the correct order—loading to loaded—and never see the unloaded state. This requires building with an "always be loading" mentality, where the default state of content in a JavaScript-enabled environment is a loading state. If you use automated testing in your development pipeline, test for these different states.

For an embarrassing example of a FOULS, look no further than my own site (**FIG 5.3**). As of this writing, I use JavaScript to dynamically load content and update the address bar without repainting the page, a technique sometimes called PJAX. This lets me use transitions between "pages" as a user navigates. But sometimes a user navigates to a part of my site that looks very different. They get the transition for unloading the page's content, but then the same content reappears right before they visit the other part of my site.

PAY ATTENTION TO FRAME RATES

Frames per second (FPS) measures how many different images can be rendered onto a surface in the space of a second. Early silent films were shown with as few as 16 FPS. Modern films are shown at 24 FPS, while in the web development community, we aim for 60 FPS. But why is this gap so wide? How can 24 FPS look fine in a movie theatre, but anything less than 60 FPS on our phones looks "janky" or choppy?

First we have to understand a little bit more about how the human eye perceives change. It can take as little as 13 milliseconds for our brains to "see" an image. That's close to 80 FPS. But we're already noticing the need for frame rates closer to 90 FPS in virtual reality development. These are much higher than the standard 60 FPS touted by performance experts as "good enough" to look smooth for the human eye. So what's happening here?

The human eye doesn't perceive "frames," it perceives motion as a continuum. One of the happy accidents of filming movies with cameras is that they also record "motion smears" that mimic this continuum. If you've ever paused an action sequence or taken hurried vacation photos, you can see these smears (**FIG 5.4**). You can show the eye a series of images with these motion blurs at a low frame rate, and it will look much more fluid than the same series without blur at a higher frame rate. Even Pixar adds motion blur to its films to help fast movements register better at low frame rates.

FIG 5.4: This young chicken was moving so fast that her leg disappeared into a smear of motion when I photographed her. When something moves quickly in our field of vision, it will stimulate a continuous smear of photoreceptors in our retina, not unlike what you see here.

On the web, we don't have motion blur. But we do have hardware constraints: 60 FPS happens to be the upper limit of what modern systems can interpret and display at a reasonable clip *today*. So we run all our animations as fast as the system will allow and hope the user won't notice. But there are cases when they will notice:

- **When moving a small graphic across a large area.** If we have a 60-foot-long screen and animate a ball moving across it at 60 FPS in the span of a second, the eyes of the audience will see 60 separate, sequential balls, appearing one after the other, one per foot. This is an extreme example of an effect called *strobing* (**FIGS 5.5A-B***)*. As web animation starts showing up on increasingly large screens, this will become an issue.

- **When the frame rate varies.** When an animation jumps from 60 FPS to 34 FPS then back again—even quickly—it can disrupt a user's flow. A 30 FPS animation that consistently runs will appear smoother than a 60 FPS animation that dips from time to time. The human visual system is always looking for inconsistencies. Inconsistencies bog down the brain.

In these instances, you may have to manually add motion blur using SVG filters or sprites and/or throttle the page's frame rate. Both techniques are beyond the scope of this book but may be worth considering for some special projects.

Alternatively, for moving graphics across large distances, you might also try fading the object out in the middle part of its trajectory, then back in at the destination. This gives the impression that the element moved so fast that it didn't register.

For the time being, try to keep your frame rate as steady as possible, either using throttling and motion blur techniques or by optimizing your performance, and be wary of moving things over large areas.

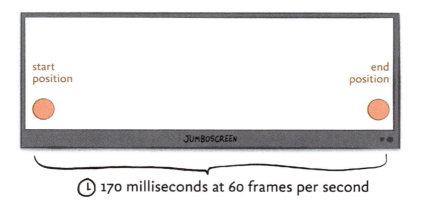

FIG 5.5A: Imagine moving an image across a large screen like a TV or a billboard in a short amount of time. At 60 FPS, the ball only has 10 frames to move from its start position to its ends position.

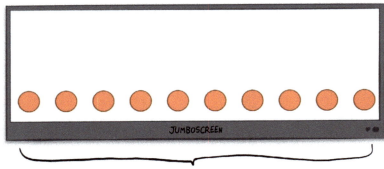

60 FPS = 10 frames per 170 milliseconds

FIG 5.5B: Ten frames mean ten individual orange balls are rendered onto the screen. The human eye is so sensitive, it will register each and every one of them. This makes the ball look like it's jumping across the space, making the animation feel janky, not smooth.

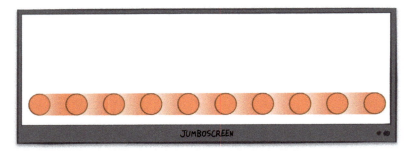

FIG 5.5C: But if we add motion blur to each of those frames, they create that "smear of motion" we saw in the image of the chicken. Although your retina can perceive change at much higher rates, this artificial smear fools your retina into seeing a more smooth and continuous motion.

RESPECT USER COGNITION DIFFERENCES

Not everyone experiences the world the same way. This has become more and more apparent in the web development and design community as we increasingly rely on user testing to try out ideas and prototypes. With animation, we must be aware of these differences—some of them are downright dangerous.

- **Time warps** occur for some people who physically experience time running faster or slower. A common example is older folks experiencing the world as racing by faster and faster while still remembering that summer seemed to last forever when they were kids. Different substances and mental states impact our perception of time, as well. Time seems to slow down for people in emergency situations, and speed up for people who are drunk. (This Wikipedia article on time perception is a fascinating place to dig in on the topic.)
- Everyone experiences time on a different scale, meaning that for some folks, the animation timings we use may seem too fast or too slow. Maybe one day, operating systems will offer time dilation controls. But until then, we can create alternate CSS with different duration values or use the Web Animations API to speed up or slow down animation playback rates across the board. Then we can let the user reduce or increase animation durations right alongside setting their motion preferences.
- **Seizures** are an increasingly concerning side effect as animation on the web becomes more common. Large, flashing red areas are the most triggering, but any on-screen change that flashes rapidly could lead to a headache, if not an outright attack. In 2008, the W3C created Web Content Accessibility Guidelines to help us build a better web for all. The current guidelines advise that elements flash no more than twice per second. Because this is a known quantity and seizures are so dangerous (and who wants to put a seizure warning on their site?), it makes sense to eliminate this kind of animation from our designs.

- **Vestibular disorders** describe a host of disorders of the human visual and balance systems. People suffering from these can have symptoms ranging from headaches to dizziness to nausea brought on by motion and animation. For some folks, a parallax effect might cause mild discomfort. For others, simply scrolling a web page can cause the room to spin. As many as 35% of Americans aged 40 years or older have experienced vestibular dysfunction in some form.

It's important to accommodate all these users, but it's impossible to design lowest common denominator animations that satisfy them all. You might be wondering if animation is worth the trouble. Those cuts are looking pretty accessible right now... But remember that the cognitive boost animation can give the majority of people is often well worth the trouble of accommodating stress cases.

Put the user in charge of their experience

Thanks to the world of operating system design, we know a bit about accommodating these folks. Remember, it's been in companies like Microsoft and Apple's best interests to make sure 100% of the population can use computers.

When iOS7 introduced zoom effects, many iPad and iPhone owners complained vociferously about dizziness. Apple developers accommodated them by releasing a patch that tucked a "reduce motion" option into the settings panel (**FIG 5.6**). This option replaced many other motion-based animations with fades, which do not trigger vestibular disorders. These options aren't limited to iOS7: earlier operating systems like Windows ME even had settings to turn off individual UI animations.

What it all comes down to is empowering our users to choose how they want to experience the web. And we can

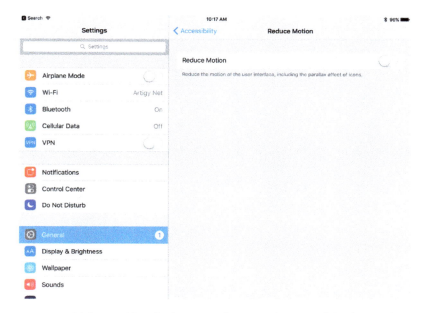

FIG 5.6: Apple's iOS provides a "Reduce Motion" option in their accessibility features that replaces the system's zooms with fades. (Watch the accompanying video.)

let those users choose for themselves whether they want full, partial, or no animation, and what speed it plays at.

We could do this with a preferences bar (a la the EU's "cookie bar"), or a settings panel shown on landing, or within the options of a web app, where we might keep other accessibility settings tucked away (FIG 5.7).

Someday browsers might offer some of these as global settings for users. There is even discussion of a "reduce motion" media query. But until then, we have options, and we *can* accommodate all users without leaving animation out of the equation.

FIG 5.7: At DevToolsChallenger.com, visitors are greeted with the option to reduce animations as well as turn on music.

a

When a user hovers over a navigation element...

b

...the navigation bar rises slightly to indicate that clicking on the menu item...

c

...will hoist a new panel onto the screen.

d

When the menu panel is open, if the user hovers over a navigation element...

e

...the panel will sink lower slightly to indicate that clicking that navigation

f

...will cause the panel to slide back off the screen.

FIG 5.8: At DevToolsChallenger.com, hovering over the menu bar option causes the bar to "lift up," signaling, "if you click me, expect me to slide further up." Hovering over the same options when it's open causes the panel to "nudge downward," saying, "if you click me, I will slide further down." (Watch the accompanying video.)

Signal oncoming animations

One thing that can be helpful for all users is signaling what things are going to animate. For instance, hovering over an expandable sidebar might cause it to slightly shift in the direction it will expand if the user clicks it (**FIG 5.8**). This sort of anticipatory animation lets users mentally prepare themselves for what happens next.

ANIMATING RESPONSIBLY

I have given you the tools you need to decide when an animation provides a solid benefit to your users and when it's a nice-to-have. You know the cost of animation to development and device performance. You know the risk involved in shipping disruptive animations to an audience with differences in their visual perception systems. Hopefully you are equipped to spot and evade trendy, unnecessary effects that will no doubt come and go just as they have since the days of Flash, from "skip intro" buttons to parallax effects.

I also want you to be wary of outdated research. It's an exciting time to be working with animation on the web. We're actively reading all the research papers that have come before in our sister industries of game and software design. But most of this research is very old and needs to be revisited.

I caution you, dear reader, against holding anything as written in stone because there was a paper published on it years ago or because someone famous has talked about it, so it must be true. I have been that person on the stage, accidentally espousing something later proven false. I would rather be challenged than put on a pedestal.

I encourage you to do your own research and share what you find. One of the strengths of our community is how eagerly and quickly we share our findings with each other, helping us all learn and iterate faster. Unlike other industries who hoard their company secrets, the web thrives on openness. We are constantly iterating, shipping, speaking, writing, tweeting, coding, forking, pushing. We share our triumphs, our research, our knowledge. We test more, iterate faster, and spread knowledge farther than anyone else. And with UI animation, we have the opportunity to uncover new discoveries and great truths, going beyond mere hackneyed rules of thumb.

This openness means that the next big breakthrough will come from someone like you, someone picking up this book and looking at it with fresh eyes. You're going to uncover new truths, truths that other communities may learn from. I look forward to the day when we can see an entire book dedicated to the science and best practices of animation for the web. Until then, may these notes serve you well.

Go forth and animate... responsibly!

ACKNOWLEDGMENTS

This book might never have come to be if it weren't for the unending encouragement and support of many people, both folks near and dear to my heart as well as people I only know through the magic of the internet. I'm surely going to leave someone out, and I hope they'll forgive me. They are wonderful people.

I'd like to personally give a shout-out to Pablo Defendini for giving me a safe place to land and cheering me on when I was considering turning back, and Sara Wachter-Boettcher for her astute and practical advice from day one.

Special thanks to the editorial team at A Book Apart, especially Lisa Maria Martin and Katel LeDû, whose input and feedback made this book more awesome than it would've been on its own. And thank you to Scott Hudson, Dennis Kramer, Amanda Phingbodhipakkiya, Amy Lee, Rachel Nash, Jason Shen, Sam Cusano, Matias Duarte, Ryan Brownhill, Heather Daggett, Michal Staniszewski, Josh Murtack, Nicholas Jitkoff, and Nat Astor for taking the time to let me ask them so many questions about motion design.

I'm grateful to Ivana McConnell for covering Web Animation Weekly when book editing took up all my time, and to Justin Cone at Motionographer for seeing the need for a book like this within the motion design community.

To my husband, thank you for being a really supportive spouse. And I mean that in the "wraps a blanket around you and puts a hot cup of something in your hand so you can keep typing while he does your chores" sort of way.

And thank you to the countless others on Twitter and Facebook, to my friends and family, and to readers of my newsletter, who have all motivated me with their questions and their eagerness to know more.

RESOURCES

THE WORLD OF WEB animation is moving fast! I run the Web Animation Weekly newsletter to help folks like you keep up.

Additionally, the Animation at Work Slack community is full of wonderful, helpful people who love this space as much as I do. It's a great place to share ideas and get feedback from some of the brightest minds in this space.

If you're keen to dig into CSS Animations and Transitions and possibly the Web Animations API, here are some great starting points:

- My course on CSS Animations and Transitions comes packed with videos and code examples.
- Are you more of a reader, less into hands-on learning? *Creating Web Animations* by Kirupa Chinnathambi is a solid, accessible book written by someone who knows the topic very well.
- If you want to get started with the Web Animations API, I have heaps of resources on the topic.

The motion design industry has many good references for onboarding aspiring motion designers. Here are two of my favorite:

- *Motion Graphics: Principles and Practices from the Ground Up* by Ian Crook and Peter Beare is a course on the topic unto itself.
- *Design for Motion* by Austin Shaw features interviews with many prominent and accomplished motion designers alongside their work.

If you want to learn more about studio animation, there are two industry staples:

- *The Illusion of Life* by Ollie Johnston and Frank Thomas is a classic, almost a style guide for the Disney way of animation.
- *The Animator's Survival Kit* by Richard Williams is a starting point for people looking to get into studio animation, covering things like walk and run cycles and practical studio animation techniques.

However insightful these books, I personally feel they are only minimally applicable to designing with animation. If you're really drawn to studio animation, I encourage you to look at some lesser-known gems. My personal library contains:

- *Tezuka School of Animation, 1: Learning the Basics* from Tezuka Productions covers the basics of animation quickly and efficiently.
- *Chuck Amuck* is another great read from one of the more famous rivals of Disney animation.
- The *"Starting/Turning Point"* books contain a lifetime of essays by possibly the greatest animator alive today, Hayao Miyazaki. When I'm stuck for inspiration, a gentle read with a cup of tea from these books gets me on track again.
- *Starting Point, 1979-1996,* Hayao Miyazaki, VIZ Media LLC, 2014
- *Starting Point, 1997-2008,* Hayao Miyazaki, VIZ Media LLC, 2014
  If you'd like to master the art and science of storyboarding:
- For a more in-depth treatise on storyboarding for the web, I wrote a guide for *net Mag*.
- If you want to go even deeper, *Storyboard Design Course* by Giuseppe Christian is an excellent guide to storyboard techniques from a film perspective.

Lots of scientific research in the field of animation and inter-action exists, some of it more applicable than others. I encourage you to keep an eye out for new and old research relevant to the field:

- *The Functional Art* by Alberto Cairo is my favorite book about data visualization, and it just so happens to have a fantastic multichapter section on the human visual system.
- *Vision and Art: the Biology of Seeing* by Margaret Livingstone is more about how images are processed by the brain and less about motion processing, but it's enjoyable and comprehensive.
- Animation Support in a User Interface Toolkit: Flexible, Robust, and Reusable Abstractions (PDF) by Scott E. Hudson and John T. Stasko is one of my favorite papers on the topic of interface animation.
- The ACM Digital Library contains a wealth of papers on all topics of human-computer interaction and computer animation.

REFERENCES

Shortened URLs are numbered sequentially; the related long URLs are listed below for reference.

Introduction

00-01 http://www.cc.gatech.edu/classes/AY2009/cs4470_fall/readings/animation.pdf

Chapter 1

01-01 https://smartech.gatech.edu/bitstream/handle/1853/3627/93-17.pdf
01-02 https://www.ncbi.nlm.nih.gov/pmc/articles/PMC3208769/
01-03 http://www.cracked.com/article_15239_the-5-most-annoying-banner-ads-internet.html

Chapter 2

02-01 https://web.nike.com/xp/sbdunk/index.html
02-02 https://www.fluevog.com
02-03 https://www.glossier.com
02-04 http://www.montereybayaquarium.org/animals-and-experiences
02-05 http://www.animalmade.com/
02-06 http://revisionisthistory.com/
02-07 https://www.polygon.com

Chapter 3

03-01 http://cubic-bezier.com/
03-02 http://easings.net/
03-03 https://www.nngroup.com/articles/response-times-3-important-limits/
03-04 https://research.googleblog.com/2009/06/speed-matters.html
03-05 https://www.doubleclickbygoogle.com/articles/mobile-speed-matters/
03-06 http://www.humanbenchmark.com/tests/reactiontime
03-07 https://en.wikipedia.org/wiki/Human_processor_model
03-08 http://alistapart.com/article/more-meaningful-typography
03-09 https://www.lightningdesignsystem.com/

Chapter 4

04-01 https://www.lightningdesignsystem.com/guidelines/motion/

04-02 goo.gl/PyBXI7

04-03 http://boords.com

Chapter 5

05-01 http://women.duluthtrading.com/

05-02 http://www.dailymail.co.uk/sciencetech/article-2542583/Scientists-record-fastest-time-human-image-takes-just-13-milliseconds.html

05-03 https://en.wikipedia.org/wiki/Time_perception

05-04 https://developer.mozilla.org/en-US/docs/Web/API/Web_Animations_API

05-05 https://www.w3.org/TR/UNDERSTANDING-WCAG20/seizure.html

05-06 http://vestibular.org/understanding-vestibular-disorder

05-07 https://github.com/w3c/csswg-drafts/issues/442

05-08 http://devtoolschallenger.com/

Resources

06-01 http://webanimationweekly.com/

06-02 http://slack.animationatwork.com/

06-03 http://rachelnabors.com/css-animations-course/

06-04 http://shop.oreilly.com/product/0636920050858.do

06-05 http://rachelnabors.com/waapi

06-06 https://www.bloomsbury.com/uk/motion-graphics-9781472569004/

06-07 http://www.routledgetextbooks.com/textbooks/9781138812093/

06-08 https://www.abebooks.com/book-search/title/the-illusion-of-life-disney-animation/

06-09 http://www.theanimatorssurvivalkit.com/

06-10 https://www.goodreads.com/book/show/969189.Tezuka_School_of_Animation_1

06-11 http://www.chuckjones.com/bugs-director-chuck-amuck/

06-12 https://www.goodreads.com/book/show/6342111-starting-point

06-13 https://www.goodreads.com/book/show/18223763-turning-point

06-14 http://www.creativebloq.com/web-design/create-storyboards-your-animations-21619177

06-15 https://www.goodreads.com/book/show/4096346-the-storyboard-design-course

06-16 http://www.thefunctionalart.com/

06-17 https://www.goodreads.com/book/show/56580.Vision_and_Art

06-18 https://smartech.gatech.edu/bitstream/handle/1853/3627/93-17.pdf

06-19 http://dl.acm.org/

Videos

INDEX

ABOUT A BOOK APART

We cover the emerging and essential topics in web design and development with style, clarity, and above all, brevity—because working designer-developers can't afford to waste time.

COLOPHON

The text is set in FF Yoga and its companion, FF Yoga Sans, both by Xavier Dupré. Headlines and cover are set in Titling Gothic by David Berlow.

Rachel Nabors began telling stories online as a teenager with her award-winning web comics. Her love of web technologies transformed into a career in front-end development, where she has worked with Mozilla, the W3C, and currently Microsoft to build the web forward. She tends the web animation community via the Animation at Work Slack and her web animation newsletter. When she isn't traveling the world, giving talks and kissing puppies, she can be found perched in Seattle, sipping a cup of fancy tea!

www.ingramcontent.com/pod-product-compliance
Lightning Source LLC
LaVergne TN
LVHW011802070326
832902LV00025B/4611